The Official

Liverpool FC Annual 2015

Written by Mark Platt

Designed by Jon Dalrymple

A Grange Publication

TM & © 2014 Liverpool FC & AG Ltd. Published by Grange Communications Ltd., Edinburgh, under licence from The Liverpool Football Club and Athletic Grounds Ltd. Printed in the EU.

Every effort has been made to ensure the accuracy of information within this publication but the publishers cannot be held responsible for any errors or omissions. Views expressed are those of the author and do not necessarily represent those of the publishers or the football club. All rights reserved.

Photography © Liverpool FC & AG Ltd and Action Images. Liverpool FC logo and crest are registered trademarks of The Liverpool Football Club and Athletic Grounds Ltd.

ISBN: 978-1-908925-67-1

£7.99

LIVERPOOL FC 2014-15
CONTENTS

LIVERPOOL FOOTBALL CLUB
HONOURS BOARD

EUROPEAN CUP/UEFA CHAMPIONS LEAGUE WINNERS

1977, 1978, 1981, 1984, 2005

FIRST DIVISION CHAMPIONS

1900/01, 1905/06, 1921/22, 1922/23, 1946/47,
1963/64, 1965/66, 1972/73, 1975/76, 1976/77,
1978/79, 1979/80, 1981/82, 1982/83, 1983/84,
1985/86, 1987/88, 1989/90

FA CUP WINNERS

1965, 1974, 1986, 1989, 1992, 2001, 2006

UEFA CUP WINNERS

1973, 1976, 2001

LEAGUE CUP WINNERS

1981, 1982, 1983, 1984, 1995, 2001, 2003, 2012

SECOND DIVISION CHAMPIONS

1893/94, 1895/96, 1904/05, 1961/62

EUROPEAN SUPER CUP/UEFA SUPER CUP WINNERS

1977, 2001, 2005

SCREENSPORT SUPER CUP WINNERS

1985/86

CHARITY/COMMUNITY SHIELD WINNERS

1964*, 1965*, 1966, 1974, 1976, 1977*, 1979, 1980, 1982,
1986*, 1988, 1989, 1990*, 2001, 2006 (*shared)

FA YOUTH CUP WINNERS

1995/96, 2005/06, 2006/07

RESERVE LEAGUE CHAMPIONS

1956/57, 1968/69, 1969/70, 1970/71, 1972/73,
1973/74, 1974/75, 1975/76, 1976/77, 1978/79,
1979/80, 1980/81, 1981/82, 1983/84, 1984/85,
1989/90, 1999/2000, 2007/08

17/8/13	STOKE CITY	(h)	FA Barclays Premier League	1-0
24/8/13	ASTON VILLA	(a)	FA Barclays Premier League	1-0
27/8/13	NOTTS COUNTY	(h)	Capital One Cup 2nd round	4-2

AUGUST

Liverpool burst out of the starting blocks in 2013/14 with August seeing them register three successive victories. In the early kick-off on the opening day of the season, Daniel Sturridge had the honour of scoring the Premier League's first goal and it was enough to clinch a slender victory at home to Stoke. It was goalkeeper Simon Mignolet though, on his competitive debut for the club, who received most of the post-match plaudits, as his late penalty save from Jonathon Walters preserved the 1-0 lead and ensured the Reds got off to a winning start. Aston Villa were then defeated by the same score-line at Villa Park the following weekend, with Sturridge again the match-winner, and a perfect month was rounded off with progress in the Capital One Cup at home to League One side Notts County, although it required extra-time before the spirited minnows were finally vanquished.

2013/14 SEASON REVIEW 2013.

This was a month that began and ended on a high but stuttered a little in the middle. September dawned with tributes being paid to the club's modern day founding father Bill Shankly in the week that he would have turned 100. On the field a well-deserved Anfield triumph over Manchester United was the perfect way in which to way to honour the great man and it meant that for the first time in 19 years Liverpool had won their opening three league games. It also established the Reds as the early season pace-setters at the top of the table but the one hundred per cent record could not be extended into a fourth game.

Victor Moses, a recent loan acquisition from Chelsea, netted on his debut in a 2-2 draw at Swansea and Southampton then inflicted a surprise home defeat on Liverpool who also bowed out of the Capital One Cup four days later, following a 1-0 defeat to Manchester United at Old Trafford. The only bright spot from that tie was the long-awaited return from suspension of Luis Suarez and it wasn't long before the Uruguayan was back among the goals, netting a double as the Reds made a welcome return to winning ways against struggling Sunderland on Wearside.

Date	Opponent		Competition	Result
1/9/13	MANCHESTER UNITED	(h)	FA Barclays Premier League	1-0
16/9/13	SWANSEA CITY	(a)	FA Barclays Premier League	2-2
21/9/13	SOUTHAMPTON	(h)	FA Barclays Premier League	0-1
25/9/13	MANCHESTER UNITED	(a)	Capital One Cup 3rd round	0-1
29/9/13	SUNDERLAND	(a)	FA Barclays Premier League	3-1

5/10/13	CRYSTAL PALACE	(h)	FA Barclays Premier League	3-1
19/10/13	NEWCASTLE UNITED	(a)	FA Barclays Premier League	2-2
26/10/13	WEST BROMWICH ALBION	(h)	FA Barclays Premier League	4-1

OCTOBER

Boosted by the timely return of Suarez, Liverpool kicked on and reaffirmed their growing credentials as title contenders by taking seven points from nine in October. Our number seven scored four times during this run, including an impressive hat-trick at home to West Brom and if that wasn't enough for opposition defences to contend with, his strike partner Daniel Sturridge also continued his prolific form with a further three goals. The SAS strike duo were suddenly the talk of the Premier League, and with captain Steven Gerrard showing no signs of ageing – scoring for the 15th successive Premier League season and becoming only the 12th Liverpool player to register over 100 league goals – a genuine feel-good factor was gradually beginning to swirl around Anfield.

With games against league leaders Arsenal and the short trip across Stanley Park to face a revitalised Everton, November always promised to be a testing month for the Reds, and so it proved. The Gunners had recently displaced Liverpool in top spot and on a disappointing evening at the Emirates it was the home side who ran out comfortable 2-0 winners. That defeat was seen as a reality check for Brendan Rodgers and his team but they bounced back in style to trounce Fulham 4-0 in front of the Kop just seven days later. With Liverpool and Everton doing well, the 222nd Merseyside derby was even more eagerly anticipated than normal and for once it fulfilled the hype. In a game that had absolutely everything, the Reds and Blues shared the points in a six-goal thriller that could have gone either way. Philippe Coutinho opened the scoring early and Suarez continued his hot-scoring streak with a stunning free-kick at the Gwladys Street End but it required a late headed equaliser from substitute Sturridge to maintain parity in a clash that will forever be remembered as one of the best in the long and illustrious history of the famous fixture.

2/11/13	ARSENAL	(a)	FA Barclays Premier League	0-2
9/11/13	FULHAM	(h)	FA Barclays Premier League	4-0
23/11/13	EVERTON	(a)	FA Barclays Premier League	3-3

DECEMBER

Despite three potentially damaging defeats, Liverpool ended the year with genuine hopes of achieving their number one objective of Champions League qualification. In a hectic month, the positives outweighed the negatives as that trio of losses were counteracted by a scintillating run of four straight victories. It began with an afternoon to forget at Hull before Suarez took it upon himself to torment Norwich once again, this time scoring four in a 5-1 midweek thrashing of the Canaries at Anfield and thus becoming the first Liverpool player to score three league hat-tricks against the same team. The goals continued to flow when West Ham visited Merseyside three days later but it wasn't just on home soil where the Reds were at their prolific best. Five goals without reply away to Tottenham was a club record win at White Hart Lane and a result that sent a tremor of fear through the Premier League. Another Suarez-inspired home win over Cardiff ensured

Liverpool were back on top for Christmas and, although 2013 ended with unlucky back-to-back defeats to fellow title rivals Manchester City and Chelsea, there was plenty for the Reds to be optimistic about as the new year loomed.

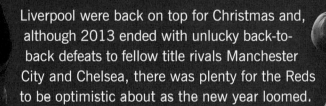

1/12/13	HULL CITY	(a)	FA Barclays Premier League	1-3
4/12/13	NORWICH CITY	(h)	FA Barclays Premier League	5-1
7/12/13	WEST HAM UNITED	(h)	FA Barclays Premier League	4-1
15/12/13	TOTTENHAM HOTSPUR	(a)	FA Barclays Premier League	5-0
21/12/13	CARDIFF CITY	(h)	FA Barclays Premier League	3-1
26/12/13	MANCHESTER CITY	(a)	FA Barclays Premier League	1-2
29/12/13	CHELSEA	(a)	FA Barclays Premier League	1-2

2013/14 SEASON REVIEW 2013.

1/1/14	HULL CITY	(h)	FA Barclays Premier League	2-0
5/1/14	OLDHAM ATHLETIC	(h)	FA Cup 3rd round	2-0
12/1/14	STOKE CITY	(a)	FA Barclays Premier League	5-3
18/1/14	ASTON VILLA	(h)	FA Barclays Premier League	2-2
25/1/14	BOURNEMOUTH	(a)	FA Cup 4th round	2-0
28/1/14	EVERTON	(h)	FA Barclays Premier League	4-0

An unbeaten start to 2014 saw Liverpool strengthen their claims for one of the highly-coveted top four places and make steady progress in the FA Cup. They welcomed in the New Year by avenging the previous month's defeat at Hull, with a routine 2-0 Anfield victory, and Iago Aspas then netted his first goal for the club in a FA Cup third round win at home to Oldham. A first ever Premier League success at the Britannia Stadium followed, with the Reds coming out on top in a spectacular 5-3 goal-fest, but a vital two points were dropped in a 2-2 home draw against Aston Villa. A place in the fifth round of the cup was guaranteed as goals from Suarez and Sturridge ended the giant-killing aspirations of Bournemouth on the south coast before Liverpool welcomed top four rivals Everton to Anfield for a game that was deemed crucial in the race for Champions League qualification. And what a game that was. The Reds were three up inside 35 minutes and threatening to run riot. When Suarez added a fourth five minutes into the second-half a record-breaking rout was on the cards. Sturridge then spurned the opportunity of a hat-trick by blazing over from the penalty spot and, much to every Evertonian's relief, there was no further scoring. Nevertheless it was a memorable night and the biggest home win over Everton since 1972 was the cause of much celebration among the red half of Merseyside.

LIVERPOOL FC 2014-15
2013/14 SEASON REVIEW

2/2/14	WEST BROMWICH ALBION	(a)	FA Barclays Premier League	1-1
8/2/14	ARSENAL	(h)	FA Barclays Premier League	5-1
12/2/14	FULHAM	(a)	FA Barclays Premier League	3-2
16/2/14	ARSENAL	(a)	FA Cup 5th round	1-2
23/2/14	SWANSEA CITY	(h)	FA Barclays Premier League	4-3

FEBRUARY

Liverpool lived up to their growing reputation as 'the team every neutral enjoyed watching' and, in the process, issued an ominous statement of intent to their Premier League competitors. The highlight of this month was undoubtedly the ruthless nature of their home victory over league leaders Arsenal. A breathtaking first half performance saw the Reds race into a sensational four goal lead inside the first 20 minutes and Arsène Wenger's side didn't know what had hit them. The final score of 5-1, while emphatic enough, did not do justice to Liverpool's overall superiority on the day but, with a top four finish now looking increasingly assured, thoughts began to turn to the bigger prize. The Gunners gained some revenge by ending Liverpool's interest in the FA Cup at the Emirates the following week but the team's new-found mantle as the game's 'great entertainers' was re-emphasised with exciting, but nail-biting, league wins away to Fulham and at home to Swansea.

2013/14 SEASON REVIEW 2013.

This was the month that Liverpudlians suddenly started to dream as five straight victories sent optimism soaring that the Reds could end their long wait for a Premier League title. It began at a venue where the Reds did not have a good track record and where many of the top teams had already struggled. But an impressive 3-0 victory over a highly-rated Southampton side set the tone for an unforgettable few weeks in which they went from strength to strength. Manchester United were then comfortably despatched by the same score-line at Old Trafford before a remarkable 6-3 win at Cardiff. Those victories on the road had whipped supporters into a frenzy of excitement and, with such passionate backing, Liverpool surged towards the top of the table. At home to relegation-threatened Sunderland the team showed their battling qualities to record a slender 2-1 win but when Tottenham ran out in front of the Kop four days later the full force of their attacking prowess was unleashed on the Londoners in an emphatic 4-0 demolition that had bookmakers hurriedly slashing their title odds.

1/3/14	SOUTHAMPTON	(a)	FA Barclays Premier League	3-0
16/3/14	MANCHESTER UNITED	(a)	FA Barclays Premier League	3-0
22/3/14	CARDIFF CITY	(a)	FA Barclays Premier League	6-3
26/3/14	SUNDERLAND	(h)	FA Barclays Premier League	2-1
30/3/14	TOTTENHAM HOTSPUR	(h)	FA Barclays Premier League	4-0

2013/14 SEASON REVIEW

6/4/14	WEST HAM UNITED	(a)	FA Barclays Premier League	2-1
13/4/14	MANCHESTER CITY	(h)	FA Barclays Premier League	3-2
20/4/14	NORWICH CITY	(a)	FA Barclays Premier League	3-2
27/4/1	CHELSEA	(h)	FA Barclays Premier League	0-2

APRIL

As the title race entered its final straight, momentum was very much with leaders Liverpool and in a month of nerve-shredding tension they moved to within touching distance of the trophy by extending their winning streak to nine games. A brace of penalties from captain Steven Gerrard secured three vital points at Upton Park and, in one of the most important league matches for decades, Philippe Coutinho settled a five-goal thriller against fellow title challengers Manchester City on an emotional afternoon when we remembered the victims of Hillsborough ahead of the impending 25th anniversary of the disaster. After Norwich were beaten on Easter Sunday the Reds needed just seven points from their final three games to be crowned champions, but an unfortunate slip by Steven Gerrard at home to Chelsea was to prove costly. It handed José Mourinho's men a fortuitous half-time lead from which, given the ultra-defensive set-up of the visitors, there was no way back. A late breakaway goal doubled the margin of this cruel defeat and,

as the destiny of the Premier League was handed back to Manchester City, the collective pain that resonated around Anfield was palpable.

2013/14 SEASON REVIEW 2013

Despite having surrendered their proud 14-game unbeaten run, for the first time since they were last champions in 1990, Liverpool entered the final month of the season still in with a shout of landing the title. To do so they had to hope that City would drop points and be ready to capitalise by winning their remaining two games. Unfortunately it was not to be. On Bank Holiday Monday at Selhurst Park they raced into a three-goal lead and looked set to crank up the pressure but a late collapse allowed Palace to snatch a draw and left Liverpudlians deflated once again. The point gained was enough to regain top spot but, with City having a game in hand, it was now going to take a catastrophic collapse for Manuel Pellegrini's side to falter. And they didn't, meaning Liverpool's 2-1 home win over Newcastle on the final day was purely academic. The overriding feeling as the players waved farewell was one of disappointment that the title had slipped from their grasp but this was a season in which Liverpool had well and truly exceeded expectations. The number one primary objective of Champions League qualification had been achieved with plenty to spare and it will be remembered as one of the most exhilarating campaigns in the club's recent history. The wait for number 19 continues but, on the evidence of what we witnessed during 2013/14, it's getting closer.

| 5/5/14 | CRYSTAL PALACE | (a) | FA Barclays Premier League | 3-3 |
| 11/5/14 | NEWCASTLE UNITED | (h) | FA Barclays Premier League | 2-1 |

Brendan Rodgers has worked wonders since taking charge of the Reds in the summer of 2012 and is laying the foundations for what every Liverpool supporter hopes will be a return to the glory days of the past.

Q Brendan, you're now just over two years into the job as Manager of Liverpool Football Club, what would be your overall assessment so far?

A The restoration when I came in two years ago was to get Liverpool back to become one of the leading clubs in Europe and over the last two years, the identity of the team and the style of football has made the British league and the European leagues sit up and take notice. Last season we had some incredible performances and I genuinely believe that we have recovered the soul of the club again for the supporters. They feel pride and enthusiasm in the club and they have a spring in their step because we are heading back in the direction of where Liverpool Football Club should be, and that's the best.

Q The 2013/14 season was certainly one no Liverpool supporter will forget in a hurry – what would you pick out as your own personal highlights of that campaign?

A We had a number of remarkable performances throughout the season. Just look at some of the scorelines - 3-0 Manchester United, 4-0 Everton, 5-1 Arsenal, 4-0 and 5-0 Tottenham. I look back on that day as the moment the players truly believed in how we work. From that day on, I saw just that one per cent change in terms of how they trained and how we could approach the games. I just think it was the one which gave the team the belief in how we had been working. We had been improving and developing really well. We had been growing as a team but I felt that was the first away game where, against a rival, we were able to demonstrate our ideas of football. Tottenham are deemed a rival and they were deemed a club ahead of where Liverpool were. Plus, the club's results at White Hart Lane hadn't been so good for a number of years. To go there and be so complete and play a perfect game in terms of how we want to pass and how we want to press, with penetration, with goals and young players in the team performing really well.

Q The club's number one objective at the start of 2013/14 was Champions League qualification. How did it feel to achieve that with games to spare?

A I think at the time, it went almost unnoticed in the media and that is a reflection of the progress we had made. This club has been after Champions League football for the last four or five years and, by the time we secured the points that made this possible, I think everyone just expected it. I take that as a compliment to myself, my staff and the players. The fact that we weren't jumping around about it afterwards also says a lot. By that stage we were being talked about as genuine contenders for the title and that is a real measure of how far we have come because at the start of the season that seemed an impossible task.

Q The season ended with you being voted Manager of the Year by the LMA, that must have been a great way to end an unforgettable campaign?

A I was extremely honored to pick up this award. I have been a manager for about five years and I remember going to my first LMA awards, and seeing the great names that had won the award in the past. You always hope that one day you have done a job worthy of all your peers. It's similar to the players' award really; the biggest compliment you can get is from the people in your own industry. Every manager across all the divisions had to make a vote and I was very proud that they voted for me and my work at Liverpool.

Q And finally, a word for the supporters and what you believe the future holds for this club?

A To finish last season with 84 points, 101 goals and 12 wins from our last 14 showed the incredible nature and quality of this team. It's given us huge belief and optimism. Both the young players and senior players will be better for the experience. Alongside this you have the passion of the supporters. What we've seen is the Liverpool of old. The banners and the flags, the lining of the streets is something I'll never forget. They have been allowed to dream and they will be able to continue doing that because we are going to get better.

Q At one stage it looked as though Liverpool were about to end their long wait for the title – what are your thoughts on that run-in now you've had more time to reflect?

A I think people looked at the last few games and asked the question "could we handle the pressure?" For me, when you win twelve games out of your last 14 in the run in, you can handle the pressure. It's unfair to look at Steven's slip at Chelsea as a real significant factor in why we didn't go on to win the league. Titles are not won or lost in one particular game; it's over the course of 38. We all shared the pain felt by the supporters that we didn't finish as champions but I feel immense pride that we were able to push right to the very end and our aim is to go one step higher next season.

LIVERPOOL FC 2014-15
15 YEARS OF STEVIE G. 15

He's been a mainstay in the Liverpool team first team for the past decade and a half; a Liverpool legend, an Anfield icon, a world-class footballer and a truly inspirational captain. Steven Gerrard graduated from Academy way back in 1998 and is now by far the longest-serving player at the club.

Last year he was voted the greatest ever to pull on the famous red shirt and his stature within the game is unquestioned. Loved by the fans, respected by his team-mates and envied by the opposition, he's a boyhood Liverpudlian who is still living the dream.

A constant driving force in the centre of the Reds midfield, he has so often been Liverpool's saviour down the years and although, at 34, he may be entering the veteran stage of his career, he still exerts a massive influence.

It's hard to imagine a Liverpool team taking to the field without him and so, to commemorate his 15 seasons in the first team, we take a look back at the illustrious career of Stevie G...

Steven Gerrard's Trophy Cabinet

Champions League (2005)

FA Cup (2001, 2006)

UEFA Cup (2001)

League Cup (2001, 2003, 2012)

Super Cup (2001)

Community Shield (2006)

FWA Player of the Year (2006)

PFA Player of the Year (2009)

1998/99
Called up to the senior squad for the first time by Gérard Houllier and handed his debut, aged 18, as a late substitute in a 2-0 home win over Blackburn Rovers.
Appearances: 13 Goals: 0

1999/00
Establishes himself as a regular in the first team and nets his first goal in a 4-1 victory at home to Sheffield Wednesday.
Appearances: 31 Goals: 1

2000/01
Plays an integral role as Liverpool complete an unprecedented cup treble, caps an unforgettable campaign by scoring in the UEFA Cup final triumph over Alavés in Dortmund and is named Young Player of the Year by the PFA.
Appearances: 50 Goals: 10

2001/02
Experiences Champions League football for the first time and scores the first of nine Merseyside derby goals.
Appearances: 45 Goals: 4

2002/03
Opens the scoring with a stunning strike against Manchester United as Liverpool win the Worthington Cup in Cardiff.
Appearances: 54 Goals: 7

2003/04
Succeeds Sami Hyypiä as Liverpool captain and wears the armband for the first time in a UEFA Cup tie at home to Olimpija Ljubljana.
Appearances: 47 Goals: 6

2004/05
Lifts his first trophy as skipper after inspiring Liverpool to Champions League glory against AC Milan in Istanbul, a game in which his goal sparked a miraculous comeback.
Appearances: 43 Goals: 13

Last 10 Liverpool captains before Gerrard

Sami Hyypiä, Robbie Fowler, Jamie Redknapp, Paul Ince, John Barnes, Ian Rush, Mark Wright, Steve Nicol, Ronnie Whelan, Alan Hansen

CAPTAIN

2005/06
Another inspirational cup final performance, this time in the FA Cup, sees him net twice in a thrilling fight-back against West Ham and also claim the PFA Player of the Year award.
Appearances: 53 Goals: 23

2006/07
Leads the Reds to another Champions League final but suffers the heartache of defeat in Athens as AC Milan avenge their loss from two years before.
Appearances: 51 Goals: 11

2007/08
Scores his 23rd European goal in a 4-0 victory away to Marseille and, in doing so, becomes Liverpool's all-time leading goalscorer in Europe.
Appearances: 52 Goals: 21

2008/09
Records his best individual goals tally for a season as Liverpool finish runners-up in the Premier League and is honoured by the country's football writers who vote him Player of the Year.
Appearances: 44 Goals: 24

2009/10
Joins an elite band of Liverpool players to have made more than 500 first team appearances for the club.
Appearances: 49 Goals: 12

2010/11
Comes off the bench to score a memorable second-half hat-trick in a Europa League tie at home to Napoli but, due to injury, features in the fewest number of games since breaking into the first team.
Appearances: 24 Goals: 8

2011/12
Scores the first hat-trick in a Merseyside derby since Ian Rush in 1982 and collects his third major trophy as captain following a penalty shoot-out win over Cardiff City in the Carling Cup final at Wembley.
Appearances: 28 Goals: 9

2012/13
Plays in all but two games of the season and becomes only the 9th player in Liverpool history to breach the 150-goal barrier for the club.
Appearances: 46 Goals: 10

2013/14
Takes over from Alex Raisbeck as the longest-serving captain in LFC history, moves to third in the club's all-time appearances list, surpasses Kenny Dalglish's total number of Liverpool goals and equals Jan Molby's record of 42 successful penalties.
Appearances: 39 Goals: 14

Liverpool's first three all-time top appearances

Ian Callaghan – 857
Jamie Carragher – 737
STEVEN GERRARD – 669

Imagine being Liverpool manager and having at your disposal every single player that has ever pulled on the famous red shirt. To say you would be spoilt for choice is an understatement. It's the ultimate selection headache but who would you choose? Which players would make it into your all-time LFC Fantasy XI?

Forwards (x 2)

Kenny Dalglish	Fernando Torres
Ian Rush	Robbie Fowler
Luis Suarez	John Aldridge
Roger Hunt	Kevin Keegan
Gordon Hodgson	Michael Owen

Left midfield

John Barnes
Billy Liddell
Peter Thompson
Ray Kennedy
Ronnie Whelan

Centre midfield (x 2)

Steven Gerrard	Jan Molby
Graeme Souness	Gary McAllister
Dietmar Hamann	Gordon Milne
Xabi Alonso	Javier Mascherano
Terry McDermott	Steve McMahon

Right midfield

Ray Houghton
Ian Callaghan
Jimmy Case
Steve McManaman
Luis Garcia

Left-back

Gerry Byrne
Alan Kennedy
John Arne Riise
Joey Jones
Alec Lindsay

Centre-back (x 2)

Alex Raisbeck	Phil Thompson
Alan Hansen	Tommy Smith
Ron Yeats	Jamie Carragher
Mark Lawrenson	Martin Škrtel
Sami Hyypiä	Emlyn Hughes

Right-back

Phil Neal
Chris Lawler
Steve Nicol
Steve Finnan
Rob Jones

Goalkeeper

Ray Clemence
Elisha Scott
Bruce Grobbelaar
Pepe Reina
Tommy Lawrence

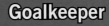

NTASY XI FANTASY XI FANTAS

There's a blank team-sheet BELOW for you to fill in but to give you a helping hand we've listed a few possible contenders for each position by looking back at some of the greatest players in the club's history on the opposite page

Don't forget though – you're the boss. The final decision is down to you and you're free to choose whatever players you wish, in whatever position you wish. The only stipulation being that they must have played at least one senior game for the club.

Challenge your friends and see who can come up with the best team. Good luck!

MY LFC FANTASY XI!

Centre forward

Centre forward

Left midfield

Centre midfield

Centre midfield

Right midfield

Left-back

Centre-back

Centre-back

Right-back

Goalkeeper

LIVERPOOL FC 2014-15
GOALS OF THE SEASON GO

In what was a record-breaking season in front of goal for Liverpool, the Reds hit the back of the net 110 times during 2013/14. Here's a countdown of the top ten...

10. Luis Suarez v Everton (h) FA Barclays Premier League: 28 January 2014 : Intercepts a pass in his own half and races clean through on goal before calmly slotting the ball past Tom Howard to complete the scoring in a memorable 4-0 win.

9. Luis Suarez v Cardiff City (h) FA Barclays Premier League: 21 December 2013 : Collects the ball on the left edge of the area and proceeds to curl a right-footed shot beyond the outstretched dive of David Marshall and into the bottom far corner to register his second of the afternoon.

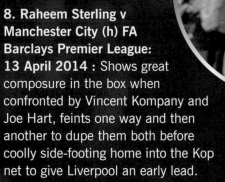

8. Raheem Sterling v Manchester City (h) FA Barclays Premier League: 13 April 2014 : Shows great composure in the box when confronted by Vincent Kompany and Joe Hart, feints one way and then another to dupe them both before coolly side-footing home into the Kop net to give Liverpool an early lead.

7. Luis Suarez v Tottenham Hotspur (a) FA Barclays Premier League: 15 December 2013 : Races on to a through ball from Luis Alberto and nonchalantly flicks the ball over the head of Hugo Lloris from the edge of the penalty area to compound Tottenham's misery with Liverpool's fourth goal in an emphatic 5-0 victory.

6. Steven Gerrard v Sunderland (h) FA Barclays Premier League: 26 March 2014 : From a free-kick on the edge of the 'D', the skipper breaks the deadlock six minutes before half-time in a tightly-fought encounter with a blistering finish into the top corner.

5. Daniel Sturridge v Everton (h) FA Barclays Premier League:
28 January 2014 : Ghosts in behind the Blues' defence to beat the offside trap and makes it 3-0 on the night with an audacious lob over the advancing Tim Howard.

4. Daniel Sturridge v West Bromwich Albion (h) FA Barclays Premier League:
26 October 2013 : Picks up possession in the opposition half and advances towards the area where, surrounded by defenders, he sublimely chips the ball into the far top corner from a seemingly impossible position.

3. Philippe Coutinho v Manchester City (h) FA Barclays Premier League: 13 April 2014 : From a corner on the right he seizes on a poor clearance by Vincent Kompany and drills a low shot into Joe Hart's bottom left-hand corner to restore Liverpool's advantage in a five-goal thriller.

2. Luis Suarez v Norwich City (h) FA Barclays Premier League: 4 December 2013 : Bearing down on goal he displays excellent control and skilfully lifts the ball over the head of one defender before unleashing a fierce strike into John Ruddy's far corner to make it 3-0 on the night.

1. Luis Suarez v Norwich City (h) FA Barclays Premier League: 4 December 2013 : For the second year running Suarez takes the award for Liverpool's goal of the season with a sensational dipping half-volley from 40-yards out that gave Canaries 'keeper John Ruddy no chance. It was his first of four in a 5-1 rout.

LIVERPOOL FC 2014-15
2014 WORLD CUP ....

The 2014 World Cup is one that will live long in the memory. For the Liverpool contingent who travelled to Brazil, however, it was a tournament of mixed emotions...

Steven Gerrard - England
Games 3   Goals 0
Eliminated at group stage

Pepe Reina - Spain
Appearances 1   Goals 0
Eliminated at group stage

Daniel Sturridge - England
Games 3   Goals 1
Eliminated at group stage

Luis Suarez - Uruguay
Games 2   Goals 2
Suspended after group stage

Glen Johnson - England
Games 2   Goals 0
Eliminated at group stage

Sebastian Coates - Uruguay
Games 1   Goals 0
Eliminated at round 16

Raheem Sterling - England
Games 3   Goals 0
Eliminated at group stage

Simon Mignolet - Belgium
Games 0   Goals 0
Eliminated at quarter-final

Jordan Henderson - England
Games 2   Goals 0
Eliminated at group stage

Mamadou Sakho - France
Games 4   Goals 0
Eliminated at quarter-final

Rickie Lambert - England
Games 1   Goals 0
Eliminated at group stage

*Adam Lallana (England), Divock Origi (Belgium) and Mario Balotelli (Italy) also featured in the 2014 World Cup but were not Liverpool players at the time.

Kolo Touré - Ivory Coast
Games 1   Goals 0
Eliminated at group stage

..SPOT THE DIFFERENCE............

Study both photographs and see if you can spot
the 12 differences. Answers on page 61.

LIVERPOOL FC 2014-15
THE BIG KOP QUIZ...............

01 In what year did Liverpool first win the FA Cup?

02 Who was the last Liverpool player before Luis Suarez to win both the Football Writers and PFA Player of the Year award in the same season?

03 Against which team did Liverpool play their opening group game in the 2004/05 Champions League?

04 True or False: Rickie Lambert has a Liver Bird tattoo on his shoulder.

05 In what year did Liverpool supporters last stand on the old Spion Kop terrace?

06 Which Australian-born defender made his Liverpool debut in December 2013?

07 Fill in the missing blanks: Rome 1977, -------, Paris 1981, --------, Brussels 1985, Istanbul 2005, -----

08 Which of these three clubs has Daniel Sturridge not played for – Bolton, Birmingham or Manchester City?

09 Who Am I? Born in Spain in 1982, I began my career with Barcelona and signed for Liverpool in 2004. I'm perhaps best remembered for what is often referred to as the 'ghost goal' and supporters still sing about me 'drinking Sangria'.

10 By what score did Liverpool suffer their heaviest ever defeat?

11 True or False: First team coach Colin Pascoe was on Liverpool's books as a youngster.

12 In which US city did Liverpool kick-off their 2014 summer tour?

13 Which of these three trophies did Liverpool not win in 1984 – Milk Cup, FA Cup or European Cup?

14 Philippe Coutinho played under which former Liverpool manager during his time at Inter Milan?

15 True or False: Manchester United once played a 'home' game at Anfield.

16 Who Am I? A boyhood Liverpudlian who experienced two spells at Everton but enjoyed my best days at Liverpool, I am one of only two players to score for both sides in the Merseyside derby and was a European Cup winner during my time at Anfield.

17 Fill in the missing blanks: Leeds 1965, -----, Everton 1986, ------, Sunderland 1992, ------, West Ham 2006.

18 At what club did Brendan Rodgers begin his senior managerial career?

19 Who were Liverpool's first ever opponents in European competition?

20 True or False: Steven Gerrard is the only Liverpool player to have scored in finals of the Champions League, UEFA Cup, FA Cup and League Cup.

21 Name the Liverpool player who was part of England's victorious World Cup final victory over West Germany in 1966?

22 From what club did Liverpool sign Raheem Sterling?

23 What Liverpool player was Zinedine Zidane talking about in 2009 when he said: "Is he the best in the world? He might not get the attention of Messi and Ronaldo but yes, I think he might be."

24 True or False: Bill Shankly won the League title as a player with Liverpool.

25 How old will Liverpool Football Club be in 2015?

WORDSEARCH

Can you find the 19 opposition teams that Liverpool will come up against in the 2014/15 FA Barclays Premier League?

Y	L	N	Q	N	F	L	G	H	Q	F	V	L	T	L	L	G	L
M	F	K	G	D	N	A	L	R	E	D	N	U	S	Q	E	C	M
A	J	Q	N	M	L	Y	K	Z	K	C	V	J	Z	V	D	O	Y
H	N	E	W	C	A	S	T	L	E	G	M	R	E	E	R	L	T
N	K	K	B	F	T	Q	K	R	S	T	A	R	T	B	J	S	I
E	M	N	R	T	C	T	P	T	L	L	T	I	T	C	K	O	C
T	L	B	T	E	Y	H	O	R	L	O	N	S	F	R	M	U	R
T	A	K	T	G	T	K	E	I	N	U	E	X	D	Y	R	T	E
O	T	E	X	J	E	S	V	L	R	W	Z	N	B	S	J	H	T
T	Z	R	S	M	Z	N	E	E	S	K	L	R	Y	T	T	A	S
J	L	B	T	N	O	C	T	C	K	E	R	K	T	A	D	M	E
Q	B	P	R	T	A	S	B	X	I	L	A	L	X	L	W	P	H
G	M	T	S	K	E	W	N	M	G	E	K	A	L	P	Y	T	C
M	L	A	V	H	N	M	S	T	T	Z	L	N	G	A	Z	O	N
P	X	N	C	L	L	U	H	H	M	B	Z	E	W	L	K	N	A
G	B	N	V	J	B	U	R	N	L	E	Y	S	N	A	H	N	M
X	A	Z	Y	V	Q	X	Q	B	D	R	V	R	Q	C	L	R	L
M	W	W	E	S	T	H	A	M	Z	R	F	A	F	E	B	G	P

Arsenal
Aston Villa
Burnley
Chelsea
Crystal Palace
Everton
Hull
Leicester
ManchesterCity
ManchesterUnited
Newcastle
QPR
Southampton
Stoke
Sunderland
Swansea
Tottenham
WestBrom
WestHam

Answers on page 61

STEVEN GERRARD

 DATE OF BIRTH

30 May 1980

BIRTHPLACE

Whiston, England

 PREVIOUS CLUBS

 SIGNED

1988 (Academy)

 LFC GAMES

669

 LFC GOALS

173

*All stats correct up until the start of the 2014/15 season

RAHEEM STERLING

DATE OF BIRTH

8 December 1994

BIRTHPLACE

Kingston, Jamaica

PREVIOUS CLUBS

Queens Park Rangers

SIGNED

February 2012

LFC GAMES

77

LFC GOALS

12

*All stats correct up until the start of the 2014/15 season

DANIEL STURRIDGE

DATE OF BIRTH

1 September 1989

BIRTHPLACE

Birmingham, England

PREVIOUS CLUBS

Manchester City, Bolton
Wanderers (loan), Chelsea

SIGNED

January 2013

LFC GAMES

49

LFC GOALS

35

*All stats correct up until the start of the 2014/15 season

PROFILES PLAYER PROFILES

SIMON MIGNOLET

DATE OF BIRTH
6 March 1988

BIRTHPLACE
Sint-Truiden, Belgium

PREVIOUS CLUBS
Sint-Truiden, Sunderland

SIGNED
June 2013

LFC GAMES
40

LFC GOALS
0

*All stats correct up until the start of the 2014/15 season

LIVERPOOL FC 2014-15
WELCOME TO LIVERPOOL

It was a busy summer in the transfer market for Liverpool manager Brendan Rodgers, who welcomed the arrival of nine major new signings. Let's meet the Anfield new boys...

Mario Balotelli

Date of birth: 12 August 1990
Birthplace: Palermo, Italy
Previous clubs: Lumezzane, Inter Milan, Manchester City, AC Milan
Signed: August 2012

Rickie Lambert

Date of birth: 16 February 1982
Birthplace: Kirkby
Previous clubs: Blackpool, Macclesfield Town, Stockport County, Rochdale, Bristol Rovers, Southampton
Signed: May 2014

Emre Can

Date of birth: 12 January 1984
Birthplace: Frankfurt, Germany
Previous clubs: Bayern Munich, Bayer Leverkusen
Signed: June 2014

Dejan Lovren

Date of birth: 5 July 1989
Birthplace: Zenica, Bosnia and Herzegovina
Previous clubs: Dinamo Zagreb, Inter Zapresic, Lyon, Southampton
Signed: July 2014

*All stats correct up until the start of the 2014/15 season

Alberto Moreno

Date of birth: 5 July 1992
Birthplace: Seville, Spain
Previous clubs: Sevilla
Signed: August 2012

Adam Lallana

Date of birth: 10 May 1988
Birthplace: St Albans
Previous clubs: Bournemouth, Southampton
Signed: July 2014

Lazar Markovic

Date of birth: 2 March 1994
Birthplace: Čačak, Serbia
Previous clubs: Partizan Belgrade, Benfica
Signed: July 2014

Divock Origi*

Date of birth: 18 April 1995
Birthplace: Ostend, Belgium
Previous clubs: Lille
Signed: August 2012
*Loaned back to Lille for the 2014/15 season

Javier Manquillo

Date of birth: 5 May 1994
Birthplace: Madrid, Spain
Previous clubs: Atletico Madrid
Signed: August 2012

*All stats correct up until the start of the 2014/15 season

Straight from the mouths of the players – what the Liverpool team had to say about the 2013/14 season....

"I'm living the dream right now, I'm on top of the world. Being back playing regularly – it's great for me. It couldn't have really gone much better. I'm really grateful for Brendan showing so much faith."

Jon Flanagan on re-establishing himself as a first-team regular.

"The most important thing for me is to give my all and do my utmost for the team. When I started out as a boy I wanted to be successful with PSG and it happened. Now I want to do the same with Liverpool. That's why I'm here."

Mamadou Sakho on fulfilling his ambitions at Anfield.

"When you score a goal, everything is blanked. You see faces; your team-mates, the opposition, the thousands of people inside the stadium. But you hear nothing. Then suddenly, the ball hits the back of the net and everything changes. I'd imagine it's like watching a game on TV without the volume then reaching for the remote when your team scores and hearing the roar. That's how it feels to me."

Raheem Sterling on the sensation of scoring a goal.

"People talk about our style of play and the passing game we like to employ with the ball at our feet. But certainly from the work we put in day in, day out, it's also about when we haven't got the ball."

Joe Allen on the style of football played by Liverpool.

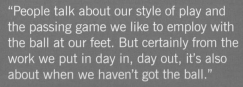

"I thought my days of title races were gone, I have to honestly admit that. But having played with this group of players this year, it's back – the dream is back. What this is going to do for this young squad is take them to the title. Whether it is next year or the year after, it will happen pretty soon – that's what I firmly believe, because the talent in the squad is there."

Steven Gerrard on why he's optimistic about the future.

"This is a fantastic club. Everyone involved here loves it and wants to get the club back where it should be. Everyone here is professional. Every time we come here we have a job to do."

Glen Johnson on life as a Liverpool player.

"I'm thankful for all the hard work and support that the fans have given us throughout the season. They've travelled with us all around England, supported us from the first minute to the very last minute. I apologise for not winning the Premier League for you guys. I'll do everything in my power, just like my team-mates will, to ensure that we do that for you next season."

Daniel Sturridge on the support of the Liverpool fans.

"There is nothing to be disappointed about. It has been a great season for the club. Nobody expected us to be where we were. I think we did everything we could but at the end City won it. We fought right until the end. What was the difference? Experience. You need the bad times to have the good times after."

Kolo Toure on why Liverpudlians have plenty of reasons to be cheerful despite not winning the league.

"To play in the Champions League is the dream for every player because it is the best competition in football and we wanted to be part of it. We worked extremely hard every single day to make sure we could achieve that."

Martin Škrtel on achieving a top four finish.

To commemorate half a century of Liverpool Football Club's participation in continental competition here's a countdown of the 50 most memorable European matches involving the Reds …

50	CSKA Moscow (Monaco)	Super Cup final 2005	won	3-1
49	Panathinaikos (h)	European Cup semi-final 1st leg 1985	won	4-0
48	Bayer Leverkusen (a)	Champions League round of 16 2nd leg 2004/05	won	3-1
47	Reykjavik (h)	European Cup Preliminary round 2nd leg 1964/65	won	6-1
46	Benfica (a)	European Cup quarter-final 1st leg 1978	won	2-1
45	Aberdeen (a)	European Cup 2nd round 1st leg 1980/81	won	1-0
44	Bayern Munich (Monaco)	Super Cup final 2001	won	3-2
43	TSV Munich 1860 (h)	Inter Cities Fairs Cup 2nd round 1st leg	won	8-0
42	Marseille (a)	Champions League group phase 2007/08	won	4-0
41	Juventus (h)	European Cup Winners' Cup 1st round 2nd leg 1965/66	won	2-0
40	Athletic Bilbao (a)	European Cup 2nd round 2nd leg 1983/84	won	1-0
39	Bayern Munich (h)	Inter Cities Fairs Cup quarter-final 1st leg 1970/71	won	3-0

38	Borussia Monchengladbach (h)	1978 European Cup semi-final 2nd leg 1977/78	won	3-0
37	Dinamo Bucureşti (a)	European Cup semi-final 2nd leg 1983/84	won	2-1
36	Aberdeen (h)	European Cup 2nd round 2nd leg 1980/81	won	4-0
35	Hamburg (h)	Super Cup final 2nd leg 1977/78	won	6-0
34	Cologne (Rotterdam)	European Cup quarter-final play-off 1964/65	drew	2-2 (won on toss of disc)
33	Besiktas (h)	Champions League group phase 2007/08	won	8-0
32	Reykjavik (a)	European Cup preliminary round 1st leg 1964/65	won	5-0
31	AS Roma (h)	Champions League 2nd Group Phase 2001/02	won	2-0
30	Anderlecht (h)	European Cup 1st round 1st leg 1964/65	won	3-0
29	Barcelona (h)	UEFA Cup semi-final 2nd leg 2000/01	won	1-0
28	Benfica (a)	European Cup quarter-final 2nd leg 1983/84	won	4-1
27	Inter Milan (a)	Champions League round of 16 2nd leg 2007/08	won	1-0
26	Barcelona (a)	Champions League round of 16 1st leg 2007	won	2-1

25	Juventus (h)	Champions League quarter-final 1st leg 2004/05	won	2-1
24	Auxerre (h)	UEFA Cup 2nd round 2nd leg 1991/92	won	3-0
23	AS Roma (a)	UEFA Cup 4th round 1st leg 2000/01	won	2-0
22	Stromsgodset Drammen (h)	European Cup Winners' Cup 1st round 1st leg 1974/75	won	11-0
21	Borussia Mönchengladbach (a)	UEFA Cup final 2nd leg 1973	lost	0-2
20	Real Madrid (a)	Champions League round of 16 1st leg 2008/09	won	1-0
19	Barcelona (a)	UEFA Cup semi-final 1st leg 1975/76	won	1-0
18	Real Madrid (h)	Champions League round of 16 2nd leg 2008/09	won	4-0
17	Arsenal (h)	Champions League quarter-final 2nd leg	won	4-2
16	FC Bruges (a)	UEFA Cup final 2nd leg 1976	drew	1-1
15	Celtic (h)	European Cup Winners' Cup semi-final 2nd leg 1965/66	won	2-0
14	Olympiacos (h)	Champions League group phase 2004/05	won	3-1
13	Bayern Munich (a)	European Cup semi-final 2nd leg 1980/81	drew	1-1

12	Borussia Mönchengladbach (h)	UEFA Cup final 1st leg 1973	won	3-0
11	FC Bruges (h)	UEFA Cup final 1st leg 1976	won	3-2
10	Chelsea (h)	Champions League semi-final 2nd leg 2006/07	won	1-0 (and 4-1 on pens)
9	FC Bruges (Wembley)	European Cup final 1978	won	1-0
8	Alaves (Dortmund)	UEFA Cup final 2001	won	5-4
7	Chelsea (h)	Champions League semi-final 2nd leg 2004/05	won	1-0
6	Real Madrid (Paris)	European Cup final 1981	won	1-0
5	Inter Milan (h)	European Cup semi-final 1st leg 1964/65	won	3-1
4	AS Roma (Rome)	European Cup final 1984	drew	1-1 (won 4-2 on pens)
3	St Etienne (h)	European Cup quarter-final 2nd leg 1976/77	won	3-1
2	Borussia Mönchengladbach (Rome)	European Cup final 1977	won	3-1
1	AC Milan (Istanbul)	Champions League final 2005	drew	3-3 (won 3-2 on pens)

GET TO KNOW...
MIGHTY RED...

Nicknames: Mighty.

Hobbies: Absolutely loves a kick-about. Riding his scooter, skateboard and BMX, computer games, going to the park, swimming, all sports. Loves writing and talking to fans on Twitter and Facebook.

Own chant: Fans have made up a chant for Mighty. Just like Sami Hyypia's but using Mighty's name. http://www.youtube.com/watch?v=LdFWLiDhilk.

Likes: Seeing Anfield full of fans, singing at game, and a pre-match milkshake.

Dislikes: Sitting still, too much homework vand Brussels sprouts!

Favourite Color: Red (of course!)

Favourite Position on the pitch: Striker, loves scoring goals but he will play anywhere as long as he gets a game!

Favourite Food: Different foods fascinate Mighty but nothing ever beats his Mum's homemade scouse and crusty bread.

Favourite Drink: Milk.

Favourite Song: "You'll Never Walk Alone" by Gerry and the Pacemakers or his entrance song "Oh Mighty Mighty" based on the football chant (melody taken from Chicory Tip - Son of my Father).

Birthday: 19th January (Liverbird adopted as the Liverpool FC emblem in 1901... therefore 19.01.

Favourite Bands: The Beatles as they are from Liverpool then current pop music like One Direction, Justin Bieber, Take That, The Wanted and Little Mix.

Favourite Pranks: He likes to get a laugh from an audience. Going to hi-five and removing his hand / tapping on one side of back and looking the other side. Placing a whoopee cushion on the seat! Fake spiders, bugs and various other creepy crawlies. Dropping water bombs!

Favourite Video Games: Any football game on his console, Mario Kart, Guitar Hero and active games like WII Water Sports.

Favourite Sayings: "massive", "brilliant", "boss", "wicked", "epic", "awesome" "top" "fab", "unreal".

Words to describe things he doesn't like: "rubbish", "stinks", "awful", "get out of here", "no need".

Favourite Heroes: Gerrard, Reina, Suarez, Dalglish.

Favourite things to do with his little sister: Telling stories and reading, racing with his cars, snap (card game) building with Lego blocks, trampoline.

Favourite places in Liverpool: Stanley Park – swings & slides and place for a kickabout.

What is Mighty Scared of? Lightning, mean animals, (loud barking dogs), scary dreams, funny noises in the night when it's dark. Halloween with scary stories and costumes!

Favourite Celebrity Fans: Mighty Red is always pleased to hear about celebrity LFC fans. He already knows that James Bond is a LFC fan, actress Angelina Jolie, singer Gary Barlow and tennis star Caroline Wozniacki. Mighty Red often tweets about them and tries to get them to connect to him too.

GLEN JOHNSON

DATE OF BIRTH

23 August 1984

BIRTHPLACE

Greenwich, England

PREVIOUS CLUBS

West Ham, Millwall (loan), Chelsea, Portsmouth

SIGNED

July 2009

LFC GAMES

173

LFC GOALS

8

*All stats correct up until the start of the 2014/15 season

PROFILES PLAYER PROFILES

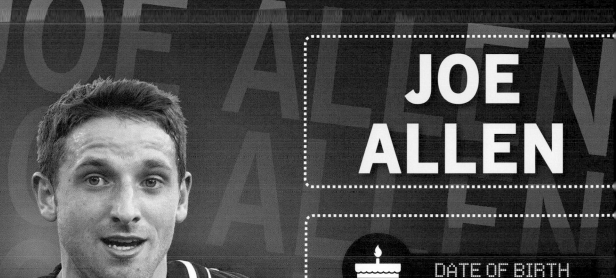

JOE ALLEN

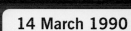

DATE OF BIRTH
14 March 1990

BIRTHPLACE

Carmarthen, Wales

PREVIOUS CLUBS

Swansea City

SIGNED

August 2012

LFC GAMES

63

LFC GOALS

3

*All stats correct up until the start of the 2014/15 season

LUCAS LEIVA

DATE OF BIRTH

9 January 1987

BIRTHPLACE

Dourados, Brazil

PREVIOUS CLUBS

Gremio

SIGNED

May 2007

LFC GAMES

243

LFC GOALS

6

*All stats correct up until the start of the 2014/15 season

JORDAN HENDERSON

 DATE OF BIRTH

17 June 1990

 BIRTHPLACE

Sunderland, England

 PREVIOUS CLUBS

Sunderland, Coventry City (loan)

 SIGNED

June 2011

 LFC GAMES

132

 LFC GOALS

13

*All stats correct up until the start of the 2014/15 season

MARTIN ŠKRTEL

DATE OF BIRTH

15 December 1984

BIRTHPLACE

Handlová, Slovakia

PREVIOUS CLUBS

FC Previdza, FC Trencin, FC Zenit

SIGNED

January 2008

LFC GAMES

246

LFC GOALS

16

*All stats correct up until the start of the 2014/15 season

PROFILES PLAYER PROFILES

PHILIPPE COUTINHO

DATE OF BIRTH
12 June 1992

BIRTHPLACE
Rio De Janeiro, Brazil

PREVIOUS CLUBS
Vasco de Gama, Inter Milan, Espanyol (loan)

SIGNED
January 2013

LFC GAMES
50

LFC GOALS
8

*All stats correct up until the start of the 2014/15 season

RICKIE LAMBERT INTERVIEW

Living the dream: Rickie Lambert is living proof that dreams can come true. In June 2014, at 32 years of age, he fulfilled his lifetime ambition and signed for the club he has supported since he was a young boy growing up in Kirkby...

As a lifelong supporter of the club, how did it feel to finally become a Liverpool player?

I couldn't believe it. I've loved this club all my life. I left here 17 years ago - and I haven't stopped loving it since. To be back here now having signed at the age of 32 is hard to describe. My mum and dad shed a few tears when I told them, especially my mum. It's not just playing for Liverpool, it's the fact I'm coming home. I've been away for eight years. My mum and dad have loved watching me play football all of my life, even when I was a kid, so it's been hard for them not being able to come and watch. The fact they've got their son home - and the fact he's playing for Liverpool - is unbelievable.

Did you ever think this day would come?

No. Obviously I had always dreamt of playing for Liverpool. It was something I always thought of when I was a kid but I did kind of think the chance of playing for them had gone. When I first heard that they were interested in signing me it was a shock but my first thought was the possibility of playing and scoring in front of the Kop.

What's been your greatest moment as a Liverpool supporter?

It's easily Istanbul. I wasn't able to go, but I went to all of the home games. The Chelsea game still stands out for me. I was on holiday with my mates and we watched it [Istanbul] - it was one of the best nights of my life, without a doubt. I think every Liverpool fan would say the same.

Your football journey is well documented - it reads like a Hollywood script. How did you keep going after facing quite a lot of rejection so young?

I just love football. Football is the only thing I cared about - it is all I thought about when I was a kid. It was all I wanted to do. When people were telling me I couldn't do it, of course I wasn't going to listen to them - I was going to find somewhere else to play football. I would have been happy playing League One, League Two, Conference... wherever. I was always going to play football. Since I have been taking it seriously and believing in myself, all my dreams, wishes and what I wanted at the start have come true in the end. It's been a long time, but it's finally come true.

RICKIE LAMBERT FACTFILE

Born:	Kirkby, Merseyside
Date of Birth:	16 February 1982
Position:	Striker
Height: 187cm	**Weight:** 76.7kg

Club career (1998-present)
580 games   233 goals

**International career
(up to World Cup 2014)**
6 caps   3 goals

RICKIE LAMBERT INTERVIEW

Because you've got that belief in yourself, does that give you confidence you'll settle in here at Liverpool?

I think I am prepared mentally now for almost anything. I've had a long career, I've experienced a lot - a lot of ups and downs - and I believe I am at a time in my life now where anything that happens, I can enjoy, get the most out of it and adapt to it. I know how big Liverpool are - and it means everything to me - but I know what is important; I know it's what I do on the pitch and the minutes I play. I know that's what matters, and that's what I'll be focused on.

Take us back to when you were at this club as a young boy and were released. How tough was that to take? I know you've said since it was the right thing at the time, but how difficult was it?

It was absolutely devastating. Absolutely devastating! I can remember at the time thinking I wasn't going to be a footballer - I'd been dropped from Liverpool and it was the end of the world for me. I was so devastated. At the time, I thought nothing was ever going to feel worse than that, but I can tell people now life goes on and you shouldn't let it hit you too much... but I never thought I'd manage to get back here!

So if you had advice for the 15-year-old you now, what would it be?

Just calm down, you are a good player and you do have a future. Just believe in yourself a little bit more.

At 32 you will be considered a veteran but is there plenty for you still to learn here at Liverpool?

Definitely. Every day I am learning - I'm 32, but I am more eager now to learn than I ever have been. It's never too late to learn. I've been with England for eight months and I've learned so much, as I have in my five years at Southampton. The development I've had has been unbelievable - and that is full credit to everyone at Southampton. The better the players you play with, the better you become, so I am sure it won't take me long to find out what their strengths are and what they like.

RICKIE LAMBERT'S CLUB CAREER

YEARS	CLUB	GAMES	GOALS
1998-2000	Blackpool	3	0
2001-02	Macclesfield	49	10
2002-05	Stockport	110	19
2005-06	Rochdale	68	28
2006-09	Bristol Rovers	115	59
2009-14	Southampton	235	117
TOTAL		580	233

LIVERPOOL FC 2014-15

THE FUTURE'S BRIGHT THE

It's been another successful year for the Liverpool Academy with impressive results on the pitch for both Neil Critchley's under-18s and Alex Inglethorpe's under-21s, plus an exciting run to the quarter-final of the FA Youth Cup. Perhaps of more significance though is the progress made by several youngsters, including this quartet who all played their way into the thoughts of first team boss Brendan Rodgers during 2013/14....

JORDAN ROSSITER

BORN: LIVERPOOL, 24 MARCH 1997

SQUAD NUMBER: 46

A promising midfielder in the Steven Gerrard mould, Rossiter has worked his way up through the Academy ranks and was elevated to the first-team squad as a 16 year-old unused substitute for the games away to Chelsea and home to Hull during the 2013/14 season. Highly rated by his peers, local lad Rossiter has made a habit of shining when playing above his age level, making his debut for the under-18s on his 15th birthday and starring in the Nextgen tournament alongside team-mates three years his senior. When captaining the under-18s he displayed great leadership qualities and, after being called up to the under-21s at 16, has not looked out of place. On the international front he has represented England in the Victory Shield and his fine progress was rewarded when handed a professional contract by Liverpool on his 17th birthday in March.

BRAD SMITH

BORN: PENRITH (AUSTRALIA), 9 APRIL 1994

SQUAD NUMBER: 44

Although born in Australia, Smith moved to Warrington whilst a teenager and was spotted by Liverpool scouts while playing for his school. An England youth international who was part of the team that reached the quarter-final of the under-17 World Cup in 2011, he was taken on the club's summer tour of North America in 2012 but later suffered a serious knee injury that sidelined him for the best part of a year. On his return to full fitness, Smith immediately impressed for the under-21s and once again caught the eye of Brendan Rodgers who drafted him into an injury hit squad for games away to Manchester City and Chelsea over the 2013 festive period. After being an unused sub at the Etihad, the fast-raiding left-back came on to make his senior debut as a 60th minute replacement for Joe Allen at Stamford Bridge. In August 2014 he joined League One side Swindon Town on loan to gain further first team experience.

CAMERON BRANNAGAN

BORN: SALFORD, 9 MAY 1996

SQUAD NUMBER: 50

A member of the club's Academy system from the tender age of eight, Brannagan may have been raised in the shadow of Old Trafford but it was the prospect of a career with the Reds of Merseyside that tempted him most and Liverpool's faith in him has certainly been vindicated so far. A goalscoring midfielder who has also proved himself more than capable of playing right-back or on the wing, Brannagan has risen impressively through the ranks at Kirkby. A regular for the under-21s and FA Youth Cup team, he signed his first professional contract with the club in November 2013 and followed in the footsteps of Smith and Rossiter when named among the substitutes for the FA Cup third round tie at home to Oldham in January.

JOAO CARLOS TEIXEIRA

BORN: BRAGA (PORTUGAL), 18 JANUARY 1993

SQUAD NUMBER: 56

A Portuguese starlet who first came to Liverpool's attention when playing against us in the Nextgen Tournament for Sporting Lisbon, Teixeira is a midfield playmaker who was signed in February 2012. His early days at the club were tempered by injury problems but, following a brief loan spell at Brentford last season, the Portugal youth international showed his potential with some eye-catching displays for Alex Inglethorpe's side in 2013/2014 and it was enough to earn him a first call-up to the senior squad for the trip to Fulham in February. Teixeira came on to replace Raheem Sterling in the 82nd minute and, with some neat touches, offered further evidence that he's got a great future ahead of him. In August 2014 he joined Championship side Brighton & Hove Albion on loan to gain further first team experience.

Under-18 stats 2013/14		Under-21 stats 2013/14		FA Youth Cup 2013/14
Neil Critchley's team finished 3rd in the under-18 FA Barclays Premier League North behind Everton and Manchester City.		Alex Inglethorpe's team finished 2nd in the regular league season before losing to Manchester United 1-0 in the semi-finals of the end of season play-offs.		**Liverpool reached the quarter-final of last season's competition**
Their overall league record was:		**Their overall league record was:**		3rd round – Blackpool **(a) 3-3, won 4-3 on pens**
Played: **31**	Won: **15**	Played: **21**	Won: **13**	4th round – Aston Villa **(h) 3-1**
Drawn: **5**	Lost: **11**	Drawn: **3**	Lost: **5**	5th round – Watford **(a) 2-0**
Goals for: **69**	Goals against: **59**	Goals for: **55**	Goals against: **30**	Quarter-final – Reading **(a) 4-4, lost 4-5 on pens**
Top scorers were Harry Wilson and Jerome Sinclair with 14 goals.		Top Scorer was Jack Dunn with 10 goals.		

LIVERPOOL FC 2014-15

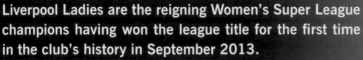
LFC LADIES LFC LADIES

Liverpool Ladies are the reigning Women's Super League champions having won the league title for the first time in the club's history in September 2013.

Following a fantastic end to the season for Matt Beard's side, the Reds beat Bristol Academy 2-0 on the final day to crown a fantastic campaign by lifting the prestigious WSL trophy.

England internationals Gemma Bonner, Lucy Bronze, Natasha Dowie and Fara Williams currently ply their trade with Liverpool Ladies, with overseas stars such as Amanda Da Costa and Corina Schroder also playing their football in the famous Red shirt.

At the 2014 PFA Player of the Year Awards, Bronze scooped the female player of the year accolade whilst her Liverpool team-mate Martha Harris took the young player prize.

Domestically, Liverpool Ladies compete in the Women's Super League alongside Arsenal Ladies, Birmingham City Ladies, Bristol Academy, Chelsea Ladies, Everton Ladies, Manchester City Women and Notts County Ladies.

Last season's Super League triumph secured European qualification for the first time and means they are now also in competition with the likes of Barcelona, Olympique Lyonnais, Paris St Germain and Wolfsburg.

The reigning WSL champions play their home games at the Select Security Stadium in Widnes - for more information you can visit liverpoolfc.com/ladies or for ticket information liverpoolfc.com/ladiestickets.

CHAMPIONS

NEVER FORGOTTEN
Hillsborough 25 Years On

On the landmark 25th anniversary of the Hillsborough tragedy, Anfield once again fell silent in a poignant service of remembrance for the Liverpool supporters who lost their lives at the 1989 FA Cup semi-final.

A quarter of a century may have now passed since Britain's worst sporting disaster plunged Merseyside into a deep state of mourning but the 96 victims have never been forgotten.

On 15 April 2014 more than 26,000 people flocked to Anfield to pay their respects. They laid tributes at the Shankly Gates before filing into all four sides of the stadium for the annual memorial service.

In a show of continued support from near neighbours Everton, the Goodison Park doors were also opened up to the public and the service shown live on big screens.

At 3.06pm a minute's silence was impeccably observed on both sides of Stanley Park, as well as across the city, with traffic coming to a standstill and pedestrians stopping in their tracks to pay their respects.

Elsewhere, Sheffield and Nottingham held their own services, while clubs from around the world were represented on the Anfield turf, where thousands of scarves donated by supporters were arranged to form the number '96'.

Liverpool embarked on their seventh tour of the United States during the summer of 2014 and despite narrowly missing out on silverware in the Guinness International Champions Cup this latest stateside visit was deemed a huge success.

The Reds received a fantastic welcome throughout their 16-day stay, with games in Boston, Chicago, New York, Charlotte and Miami attracting almost a quarter of a million supporters.

On the field, they opened with an unfortunate last-gasp friendly defeat to AS Roma at Fenway Park before moving on to the historic Soldier Field to begin their participation in the International Champions Cup, where an early Raheem Sterling goal was enough to secure a 1-0 win over Olympiacos.

Yet another iconic setting was the venue for the next game and, in a predominantly 'Red' Yankee Stadium, Premier League rivals Manchester City were overcome on penalties following a 2-2 draw after 90 minutes.

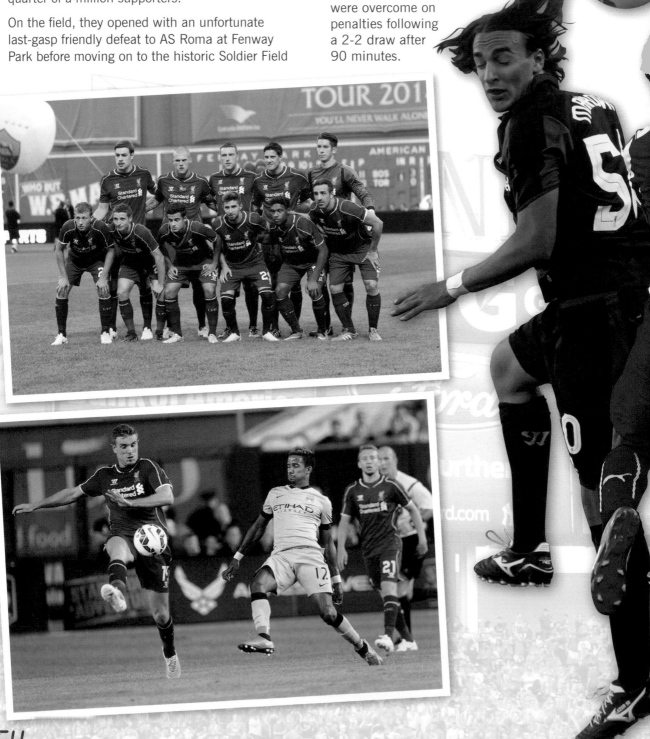

Sterling was again on the score-sheet, as was Jordan Henderson, while the shoot-out was settled by a Lucas Leiva spot-kick.

By the time Liverpool ran out to face AC Milan in Charlotte their place in the final of the tournament was assured and they completed their group fixtures with an impressive 2-0 victory over AC Milan, courtesy of goals from Joe Allen and Suso.

Manchester United were the opponents in the final at Miami's Sun Life Stadium but despite leading at the interval through a Steven Gerrard penalty the gruelling tour schedule finally told and United hit back to claim the trophy.

Nevertheless, it had been a memorable trip, providing ideal pre-season preparation for Brendan Rodgers and his team, while, at the same time, expanding further Liverpool's ever-increasing popularity in America.

"The tour was a great success," claimed the club's chief commercial officer Billy Hogan. "Our goal was always to reach the final and we achieved that. The crowds, especially in Charlotte and New York, were incredible. We have over 20 million fans across the country.

"The tour was another reminder of what an enormous club Liverpool is. It was an opportunity to bring the club closer to the fans. When you see not only the size of the crowds but the balance of the crowd at a place like Yankee Stadium, where it was significantly red, people will see - particularly in the US - the size and strength of our fan base."

"There are still a lot of great cities there that we haven't visited yet. From our perspective we will certainly be back again."

Liverpool's 2014 Summer Tour

AS Roma	Fenway Park, Boston	0-1
Olympiacos	Soldier Field, Chicago	1-0
Manchester City	Yankee Stadium, New York	2-2
		(3-1 on penalties)
AC Milan	Bank of America Stadium, Charlotte	2-0
Manchester United	Sun Life Stadium, Miami	1-3

Appearances	PL	FA	LC	Total
Jordan Henderson	35	3	2	40
Simon Mignolet	38	0	2	40
Steven Gerrard	34	3	2	39
Martin Škrtel	36	2	1	39
Raheem Sterling	33	3	2	38
Luis Suarez	33	3	1	37
Philippe Coutinho	33	3	1	37
Daniel Sturridge	29	2	2	33
Glen Johnson	29	0	1	30
Lucas Leiva	27	1	1	29
Joe Allen	24	1	1	26
Jon Flanagan	23	2	0	25
Kolo Touré	20	2	2	24
Daniel Agger	20	2	1	23
Victor Moses	19	2	1	22
Mamadou Sakho	18	0	1	19
Aly Cissokho	15	3	1	19
Iago Aspas	14	1	0	15
Luis Alberto	9	2	1	12
Jose Enrique	8	0	1	9
Martin Kelly	5	2	1	8
Brad Jones	0	3	0	3
Andre Wisdom	2	0	1	3
Jordon Ibe	1	0	1	2
Brad Smith	1	0	0	1
João Carlos Teixeira	1	0	0	1
Jordan Rossiter	0	0	0	0
Cameron Brannagan	0	0	0	0
Tiago Ilori	0	0	0	0
Stephen Sama	0	0	0	0
Danny Ward	0	0	0	0
Fabio Borini	0	0	0	0

Debutants

The following players made their Liverpool first team debuts during 2013/14...

Simon Mignolet (1)
17 August 2013
v Stoke City (h)

Kolo Touré
17 August 2013
v Stoke City (h)

Iago Aspas
17 August 2013
v Stoke City (h)

Aly Cissokho (2)
24 August 2013
v Aston Villa (a)

Luis Alberto (3)
27 August 2013
v Notts County (h)

Mamadou Sakho
16 September 2013
v Swansea City (a)

Victor Moses (4)
16 September 2013
v Swansea City (a)

Brad Smith (5)
29 December 2013
v Chelsea (a)

João Carlos Teixeira
12 February 2014
v Fulham (a)

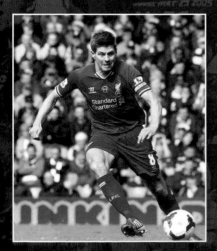

Goalscorers	PL	FA	LC	Total
Luis Suarez	31	0	0	31
Daniel Sturridge	21	2	1	24
Steven Gerrard	13	0	1	14
Raheem Sterling	9	1	0	10
Martin Škrtel	7	0	0	7
Own goals	5	0	1	6
Philippe Coutinho	5	0	0	5
Jordan Henderson	4	1	0	5
Victor Moses	1	0	1	2
Daniel Agger	2	0	0	2
Joe Allen	1	0	0	1
Jon Flanagan	1	0	0	1
Iago Aspas	0	0	1	1
Mamadou Sakho	1	0	0	1

Liverpool registered a total of 110 goals during 2013/14, split as follows...

League – 101 (a record for the club in the top-flight and their most since 106 in 1895-96)

FA Cup – 5 League Cup – 4

Assists	No
Suarez	29
Gerrard	17
Sterling	9
Coutinho, Sturridge, Henderson	8
Johnson	4
Enrique, Touré	3
Cissokho	2
Aspas, Škrtel, Agger, Ibe, Alberto, Allen	1

Liverpool's...	No.
... highest league position during 2013/14	1st
... lowest league position during 2012/13	7th
... final Premier League finishing position	2nd
... final Premier League points tally (club's best since 2008/09)	84
... biggest win (away to Tottenham Hotspur)	5-0
... highest-scoring fixture (away win to Cardiff City)	6-3
... heaviest defeat (away to Hull City)	1-3
... average home attendance	44,527

Transfers In		
Player	From	Date
Luis Alberto	Sevilla	22 June 2013
Iago Aspas	Celta Vigo	23 June 2013
Simon Mignolet	Sunderland	25 June 2013
Kolo Touré	Free	2 July 2013
Aly Cissokho (on loan)	Valencia	20 August 2013
Mamadou Sakho	PSG	2 September 2013
Tiago Ilori	Sporting Lisbon	2 September 2013
Victor Moses (on loan)	Chelsea	2 September 2013

Transfers Out		
Player	From	Date
Peter Gulasci	Red Bull Salzburg	7 June 2013
Andy Carroll	West Ham United	19 June 2013
Jonjo Shelvey	Swansea City	3 July 2013
Jay Spearing	Bolton Wanderers	9 August 2013
Stewart Downing	West Ham United	13 August 2013
Dani Pacheco	Alcorcorn	2 September 2013
Adam Morgan	Yeovil Town	2 January 2014

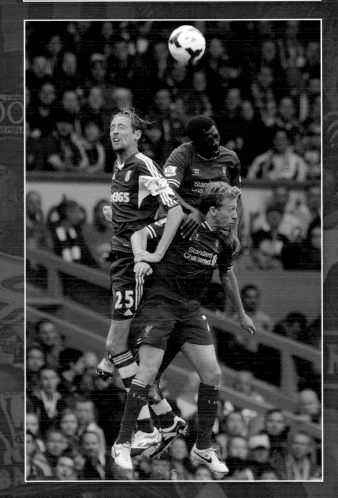

???

See you if you can guess the 3 former great Liverpool players in each of the montages below. You might need Dad to help you with this one! Answers on p60.

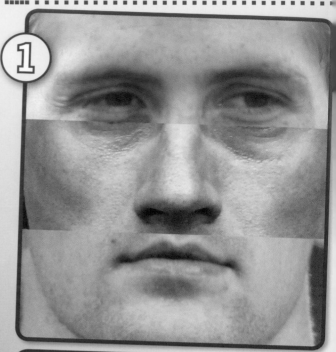

1

TOP: ....

MIDDLE: ....

BOTTOM: ....

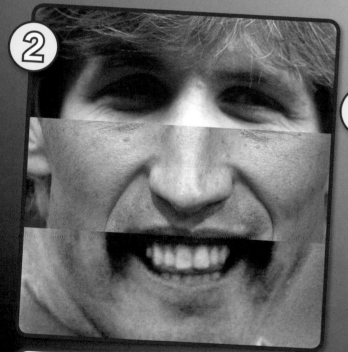

2

TOP: ....

MIDDLE: ....

BOTTOM: ....

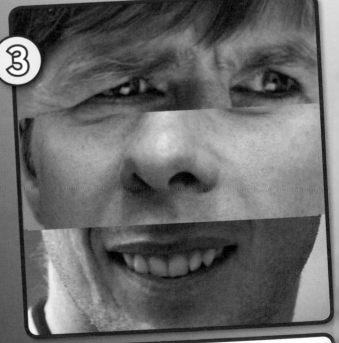

3

TOP: ....

MIDDLE: ....

BOTTOM: ....

58

..LFC SHIRT COMPETITION.........

Answer the following question correctly and you could win a Liverpool FC shirt signed by a first team player.

In what year did Liverpool first play in the famous all-red kit?

a. 1945
b. 1964
c. 1977

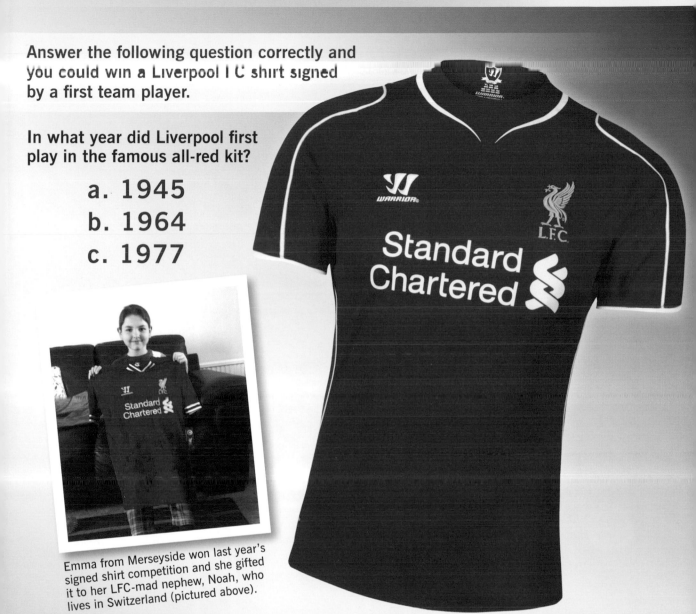

Emma from Merseyside won last year's signed shirt competition and she gifted it to her LFC-mad nephew, Noah, who lives in Switzerland (pictured above).

Entry is by email only. Only one entry per contestant. Please enter LFC SHIRT followed by either A, B or C in the subject line of an email. In the body of the email, please include your full name, address, postcode, email address and phone number and send to: frontdesk@grangecommunications.co.uk by Friday 27 March 2015.

Terms and conditions

(1) The closing date for this competition is Friday 27th March 2015 at midnight. Entries received after that time will not be counted. (2) Information on how to enter and on the prize form part of these conditions. (3) Entry is open to those residing in the UK only. If entrants are under 18, consent from a parent or guardian must be obtained and the parent or guardian must agree to these terms and conditions. (4) This competition is not open to employees or their relatives of Liverpool Football Club. Any such entries will be invalid. (5) The start date for entries is 31st October 2014 at 4pm. (6) Entries must be strictly in accordance with these terms and conditions. Any entry not in strict accordance with these terms and conditions will be deemed to be invalid and no prize will be awarded in respect of such entry. By entering, all entrants will be deemed to accept these rules. (7) One (1) lucky winner will win a 2014/15 season signed football shirt. (8) The prize is non-transferable and no cash alternative will be offered. Entry is by email only. Only one entry per contestant. Please enter LFC SHIRT followed by either A, B or C in the subject line of an email. In the body of the email, please include your full name, address, postcode, email address and phone number and send to: frontdesk@grangecommunications.co.uk by Friday 27 March 2015. (9) The winner will be picked at random. The winner will be contacted within 72 hours of the closing date. Details of the winner can be requested after this time from the address below. (10) Entries must not be sent in through agents or third parties. No responsibility can be accepted for lost, delayed, incomplete, or for electronic entries or winning notifications that are not received or delivered. Any such entries will be deemed void. (11) The winner will have 72 hours to claim their prize once initial contact has been made by the Promoter. Failure to respond may result in forfeiture of the prize. (12) On entering the competition you are allowing Liverpool Football Club and its trusted partners to contact you with information about products and services they believe might be of interest to you. If you do not wish to receive any marketing information from the Club, you can opt out by emailing LFC STOP to frontdesk@grangecommunications.co.uk before midnight on Friday 27th March 2015. (13) The Promoter reserves the right to withdraw or amend the promotion as necessary due to circumstances outside its reasonable control. The Promoter's decision on all matters is final and no correspondence will be entered into. (14) The Promoter (or any third party nominated by the Promoter) may use the winner's name and image and their comments relating to the prize for future promotional, marketing and publicity purposes in any media worldwide without notice and without any fee being paid. (15) Liverpool Football Club's decision is final, no correspondence will be entered in to. Except in respect of death or personal injury resulting from any negligence of the Club, neither Liverpool Football Club nor any of its officers, employees or agents shall be responsible for (whether in tort, contract or otherwise): (i) any loss, damage or injury to you and/or any guest or to any property belonging to you or any guest in connection with this competition and/or the prize, resulting from any cause whatsoever; (ii) for any loss of profit, loss of use, loss of opportunity or any indirect, economic or consequential losses whatsoever. (15) This competition shall be governed by English law. (16) Promoter: Grange Communications Ltd, 22 Great King Street, Edinburgh EH3 6QH.

The Big KOP Quiz Solution

1. 1965
2. John Barnes
3. Monaco
4. True
5. 1994
6. Brad Smith
7. Wembley 1978, Rome 1984, Athens 2007
8. Birmingham
9. Luis Garcia
10. 1-9
11. False
12. Boston
13. FA Cup
14. Rafael Benitez
15. True
16. David Johnson
17. Newcastle 1974, Everton 1989, Arsenal 2001
18. Watford
19. KR Reykjavik
20. True
21. Roger Hunt
22. Queens Park Rangers
23. Steven Gerrard
24. False
25. 123

Picture Puzzle Solution

Fernando Torres

Jamie Carragher

Michael Owen

Jan Molby

Sami Hyypiä

Bruce Grobbelaar

Kenny Dalglish

Xabi Alonso

Alan Hansen

Spot the Difference Solution

Wordsearch Solution

Y	L	N	Q	N	F	L	G	H	Q	F	V	L	T	L	L	G	L
M	F	K	G	D	N	A	L	R	E	D	N	U	S	Q	E	C	M
A	J	Q	N	M	L	Y	K	Z	K	C	V	J	Z	V	D	O	Y
H	N	E	W	C	A	S	T	L	E	G	M	R	E	E	R	L	T
N	K	K	B	F	T	Q	K	R	S	T	A	R	T	B	J	S	I
E	M	N	R	T	C	T	P	T	L	L	T	I	T	C	K	O	C
T	L	B	T	E	Y	H	O	R	L	O	N	S	F	R	M	U	R
T	A	K	T	G	T	K	E	I	N	U	E	X	D	Y	R	T	E
O	T	E	X	J	E	S	V	L	R	W	Z	N	B	S	J	H	T
T	Z	R	S	M	Z	N	E	E	S	K	L	R	Y	T	T	A	S
J	L	B	T	N	O	C	T	C	K	E	R	K	T	A	D	M	E
Q	B	P	R	T	A	S	B	X	I	L	A	L	X	L	W	P	H
G	M	T	S	K	E	W	N	M	G	E	K	A	L	P	Y	T	C
M	L	A	V	H	N	M	S	T	T	Z	L	N	G	A	Z	O	N
P	X	N	C	L	L	U	H	H	M	B	Z	E	W	L	K	N	A
G	B	N	V	J	B	U	R	N	L	E	Y	S	N	V	H	N	M
X	A	Z	Y	V	Q	X	Q	B	D	R	V	R	Q	C	L	R	L
M	W	W	E	S	T	H	A	M	Z	R	F	A	F	E	B	G	P

Arsenal
Aston Villa
Burnley
Chelsea
Crystal Palace
Everton
Hull
Leicester
ManchesterCity
ManchesterUnited
Newcastle
QPR
Southampton
Stoke
Sunderland
Swansea
Tottenham
WestBrom
WestHam